Contributing Author

Kassie Lewis

Editorial Project Manager

Mara Ellen Guckian

Managing Editors

Karen J. Goldfluss M.S. Ed.

Ina Masser Levin, M.A.

Illustrator

Kevin Barnes

Reneé Christine Yates

Art Manager

Kevin Barnes

Cover Design

Kevin Barnes

CJae Froshay

Art Director

CJae Froshay

Imaging

Craig L. Gunnell

Ralph Olmedo, Jr.

Publisher

Mary D. Smith, M.S. Ed.

Author

Renee Liles

Teacher Created Resources, Inc.

6421 Industry Way

Westminster, CA 92683

www.teachercreated.com.

ISBN-1-4206-3175-6

©2005 Teacher Created Resources, Inc.

Reprinted, 2006

Made in U.S.A.

Table of Contents

Table of Contents (cont.)

Introduction

Many of the most frequently used words in the English language, called *sight words*, do not follow standard decoding rules. Word flash cards help, but research has proven that young students learn best with hands-on practice. This simple, easy-to-use book will give students much-needed practice recognizing common sight words and using them to create sentences. In *Literacy Activities: Sight Words & Sentences*, students will have fun learning to read.

Using this book will help students practice reading from left-to-right when arranging words to form sentences. The color cards and puzzle-like quality of the activities will engage students and make learning to read more fun. The words are arranged in groups or themes such as animal words, family words, number words, shape and position words, action words, and question words.

Students practice with picture and word cards by matching, playing concentration, and reviewing. To further their mastery, students will use center activities and practice sheets that reinforce specific sight words. Additional activities included in each section reinforce fine motor skill development by having students cut, paste, sort, and print.

With full-color sentence cards, students begin constructing sentences. When these sight words are mastered, students can read related mini books. Finally, students can create their own sentences on special stationery with all of their newly mastered sight words.

How to Use This Book

The six sections in this book include similar activities. The specific words used in this book are listed in groups on page six. The activities and their uses are explained in detail on the following page. The full-color pages are intended for direct use as center activities in the classroom. However, the teacher may choose to copy them before creating the center cards. The full-color pages once copied, can be used for individual students. Full-color pages include Word and Picture Cards, Sentence Cards, and Mini Books.

Cards can be used in a variety of ways:

- Cards can be laminated, and the word cards at the bottom can be cut off and separated. Place each prepared card and the individual word cards in an envelope or resealable bag. Store the cards in the center in a box or other container. Students can take turns arranging the words in the correct order in the boxes provided. Advise students to note capitalization at the beginning of each sentence and punctuation at the end of each sentence.

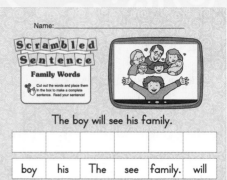

- To use the card as a worksheet in a center, copy the page and laminate it or put it in a page protector. Have students write the appropriate answers on the laminate or the page protector using thin, dry-erase pens. Wipe the card with a damp paper towel to erase when completed. Using these worksheets as part of a center allows many student opportunities to succeed at the task.

- Card pages can be copied for student use as reinforcement activities or as homework extensions. Name lines and student-friendly directions have been included on each page. Students can cut out the words and glue them in the boxes provided, or they can use the words at the bottom of the page as guides and write them in the boxes.

Activities to Learn Sight Words

Picture and Word Cards

To expose students to the basic words in each category that will help them read and write simple sentences, two sets of cards are included. The first set (pages 7, 35, 63, 91, and 119) is printed with word and picture back-to-back. Cut the cards out and laminate them. These cards can be used independently, in pairs, or in small groups. Looking at the word, the student can read it and then self-check by looking at the picture on the flip side. Looking at the picture side, the student can practice spelling the word and flip to check for accuracy by looking at the word.

Additional sets of cards (pages 9, 11, 37, 39, 65, 67, 91, 93, 121, 123, 147, and 149) have the words on one card and the pictures on another. Cut these cards out and laminate them. These cards can be used independently, in pairs, or in small groups for simple matching or in a game of Concentration.

Match Up

The Match Up cards (pages 13, 41, 69, 97, and 125) with green backgrounds are for use in a center. Prepare the page by cutting out the words and laminating them. You may also laminate the page or simply place it in a page protector. The reproducible versions of the Match Up cards have yellow backgrounds (pages 15, 43, 71, 99, and 127) are for students to use independently at school or at home.

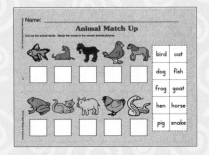

Practice Sheets

The practice sheets are intended for independent student use. However, if a student finds it too challenging, pair him or her with another student for practice. Copy the page and prepare it for center use by coloring, cutting appropriate pieces, laminating or placing in a page protector, and supplying appropriate wipe-off markers an/or cover-up pieces.

Scrambled Sentences

The Scrambled Sentence pages were designed for center or individual use. For center use, cut off the name line and cut out the word cards. Laminate the pieces and store them in individual resealable bags. Another option is to place the sentence card in a page protector and have students use wipe-off markers to complete the sentence. Copies of the pages can also be made for individual assignments.

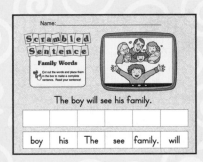

Stationery

Writing paper is provided at the end of the book for each of the themes. Use the paper to encourage students to create sentences with the words they have mastered!

Mini Books

Cut out the pages of the practice books (pages 29–33, 57–61, 85–89, 113–117, 141–145, and 165–169), laminate each page, and staple pages together. (A book binder using plastic spirals or hole punch and paper fasteners or rings can also be used.) Place the mini books in a center for students to practice reading.

Sight Words

Animal Words

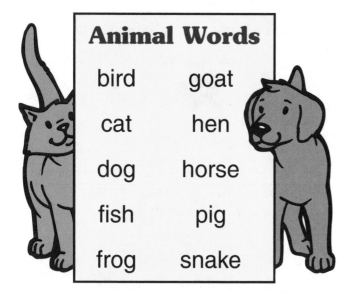

bird	goat
cat	hen
dog	horse
fish	pig
frog	snake

Family Words

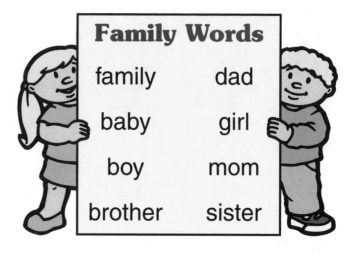

family	dad
baby	girl
boy	mom
brother	sister

Number Words

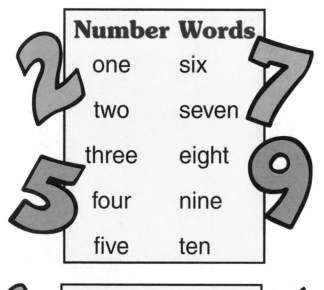

one	six
two	seven
three	eight
four	nine
five	ten

Shape and Position Words

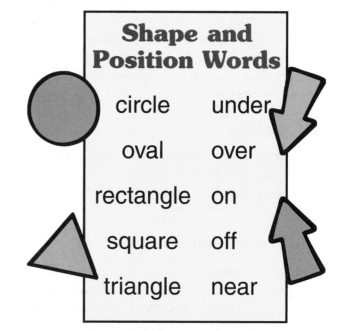

circle	under
oval	over
rectangle	on
square	off
triangle	near

Action Words

draw	run
jump	sing
look	sit
play	walk
read	write

Question Words

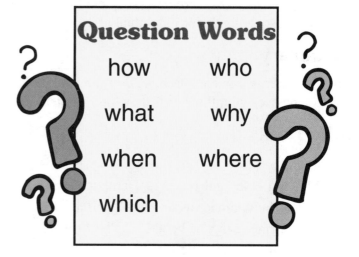

how	who
what	why
when	where
which	

Animal Picture and Word Cards

Animal Picture and Word Cards

cat

bird

fish

dog

goat

frog

horse

hen

snake

pig

Animal Picture Cards

©Teacher Created Resources, Inc.

#3175 Sight Words & Sentences

Animal Word Cards

bird	cat
dog	fish
frog	goat
hen	horse
pig	snake

Name: _____

Animal Match Up

Cut out the animal words. Match the words to the correct animal pictures.

cat	fish	goat	horse	snake
bird	dog	frog	hen	pig

14

Animal Match Up

Cut out the animal words. Glue the words under the correct animal pictures. Color the animals.

| cat | fish | goat | horse | snake |
| bird | dog | frog | hen | pig |

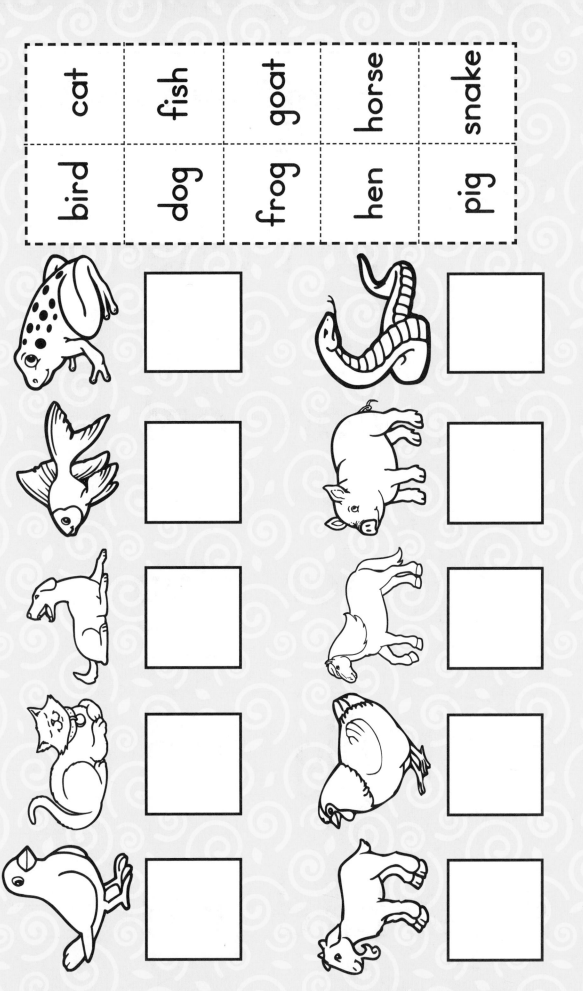

Name: _____

What Do You Call This?

Circle the animal word that names each animal picture. Write the correct animal word.

 hen when _____

 can cat _____

 dot dog _____

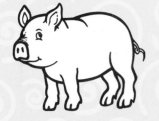 pig pin _____

 bird bid _____

Name: _____

What Do You Call That?

Circle the animal word that names each animal picture. Write the correct animal word.

 fish   fin _____

 goat   got _____

 horse hose _____

 frog   fog _____

 snake sack _____

Give It Some Color!

Color Key

| horse = gray | bird = blue |
| dog = brown | cat = orange |

Use the key to color the animals.
Fill in the blanks to complete each sentence.

This _____ is _____ .

This _____ is _____ .

This _____ is _____ .

This _____ is _____ .

18

Name: _____

Animal Words

Cut out the words and place them in the boxes to make a complete sentence. Read your sentence!

I see a blue bird.

blue	a	see	I	bird.

20

Name: _____

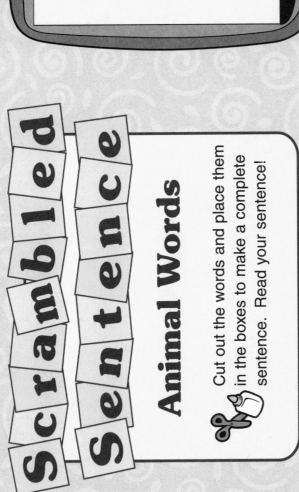

Scrambled Sentence

Animal Words

Cut out the words and place them in the boxes to make a complete sentence. Read your sentence!

The pig is pink.

The	pig	is	pink.

Name: _____

Animal Words

Cut out the words and place them in the boxes to make a complete sentence. Read your sentence!

Can you see his fish?

Can	you	his	fish?	see

24

Name: _____

Animal Words

Cut out the words and place them in the boxes to make a complete sentence. Read your sentence!

A hen can be red or black.

	or
	be
	can
	red
	black.
	A
	hen

Name: _____

Scrambled Sentence

Animal Words

Cut out the words and place them in the boxes to make a complete sentence. Read your sentence!

All of their cats are orange.

of	their	orange.	All	cats	are

28

1

I see a blue bird.

3

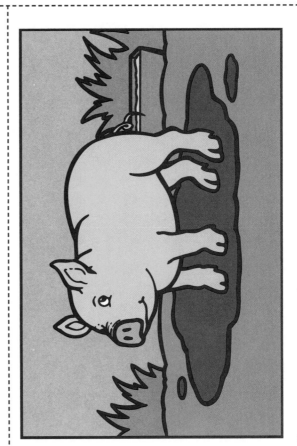

I see a pink pig.

See the Animals

By: _____

2

I see a brown dog.

5 ___

I see a purple fish.

7 ___

I see a red hen.

4 ___

I see an orange cat.

6 ___

I see a black goat.

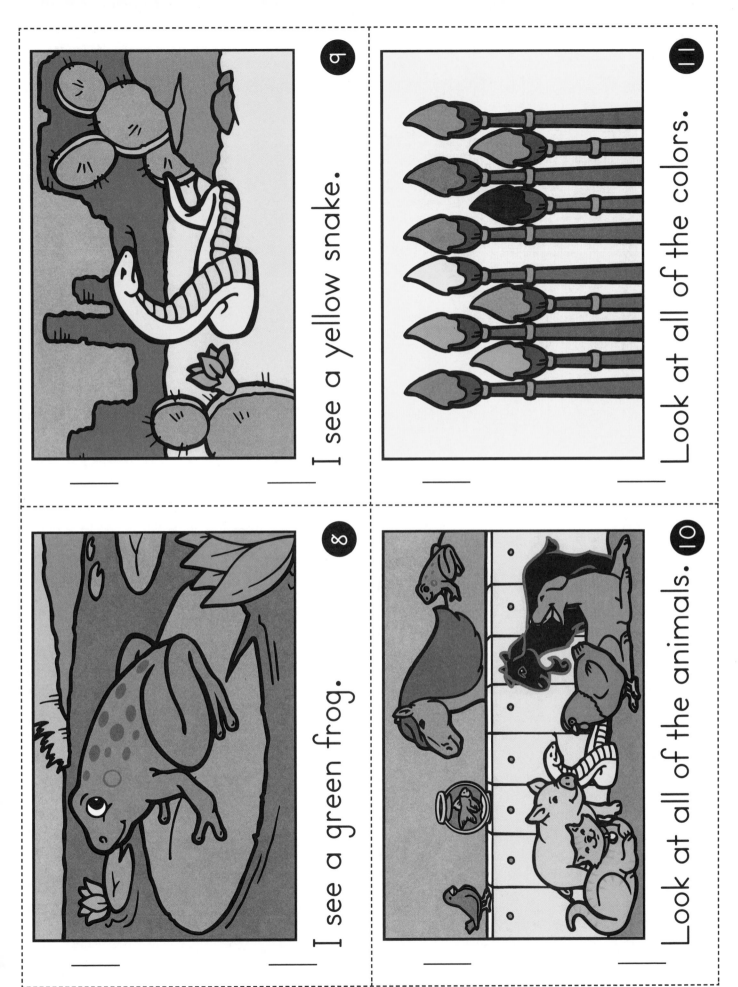

9

I see a yellow snake.

11

Look at all of the colors.

8

I see a green frog.

10

Look at all of the animals.

#3175 Sight Words & Sentences

34

Family Picture and Word Cards

Family Picture and Word Cards

dad

family

girl

baby

mom

boy

sister

brother

Family Picture Cards

Family Word Cards

family

dad

baby

girl

boy

mom

brother

sister

Family Match Up

Cut out the family words. Match the words to the correct family pictures.

baby	family
brother	boy
girl	dad
sister	mom

42

Family Match Up

Cut out the family words. Glue the words under the correct family pictures.

baby	family
brother	boy
girl	dad
sister	mom

Name: _____

Boy or Girl?

Trace the word next to the family picture with the correct family word.
Fill in the final blank of the sentence with the word *boy* or *girl*.

| mom | brother | sister | dad | boy | girl |

 A <u>mom</u> is a _____.

 A <u>brother</u> is a _____.

A <u>sister</u> is a _____.

 A <u>dad</u> is a _____.

Family Names

Circle the two words in the row that are the same.
Write the family word.

brother   brother   other   ------------

bad   dad   dad   ------------

sister   mister   sister   ------------

mom   mom   more   ------------

box   boy   boy   ------------

grill   girl   girl   ------------

Name:_____

My Family

Use the family words to write a sentence. Draw a picture of your family.

family	baby	boy	brother
dad	girl	mom	sister

Name: _____

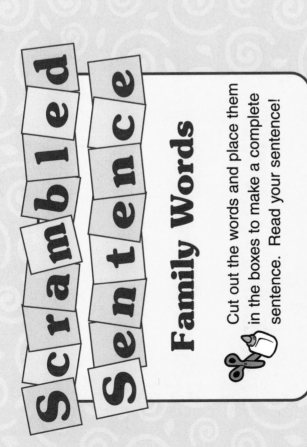

Family Words

Cut out the words and place them in the boxes to make a complete sentence. Read your sentence!

This is my brother.

my	is	This	brother.

48

Name: _____

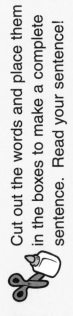

Family Words

Cut out the words and place them in the boxes to make a complete sentence. Read your sentence!

That baby is not a boy.

baby	That	boy.	a	not	is

Name: _____

Scrambled Sentence

Family Words

Cut out the words and place them in the boxes to make a complete sentence. Read your sentence!

Mom and Dad are here.

here.	Mom	Dad	and	are

52

Name: _____

Scrambled Sentence

Family Words

Cut out the words and place them in the boxes to make a complete sentence. Read your sentence!

The girls are sisters.

are	The	sisters.	girls

54

Name: _____

Scrambled
Sentence

Family Words

Cut out the words and place them in the boxes to make a complete sentence. Read your sentence!

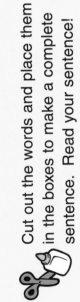

The boy will see his family.

boy	his	The	see	family.	will

56

Families

By: _____

There are many families.

___ **1**

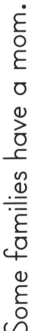

Some families have a dad.

___ **3**

Some families have a mom.

___ **2**

58

There can be boys in a family.

Some families have a sister.

Some families have a baby.

Some families have a brother.

60

9

Families can be big.

11

Who is in your family?

8

There can be girls in a family.

10

Families can be small.

62

Number Picture and Word Cards

1

2

3

4

5

6

7

8

9

10

Number Picture and Word Cards

two

one

four

three

six

five

eight

seven

ten

nine

Number Picture Cards

1

2

3

4

5

6

7

8

9

10

Number Word Cards

one	two
three	four
five	six
seven	eight
nine	ten

Name:

Number Match Up

Cut out the number words and match them to the correct number pictures.

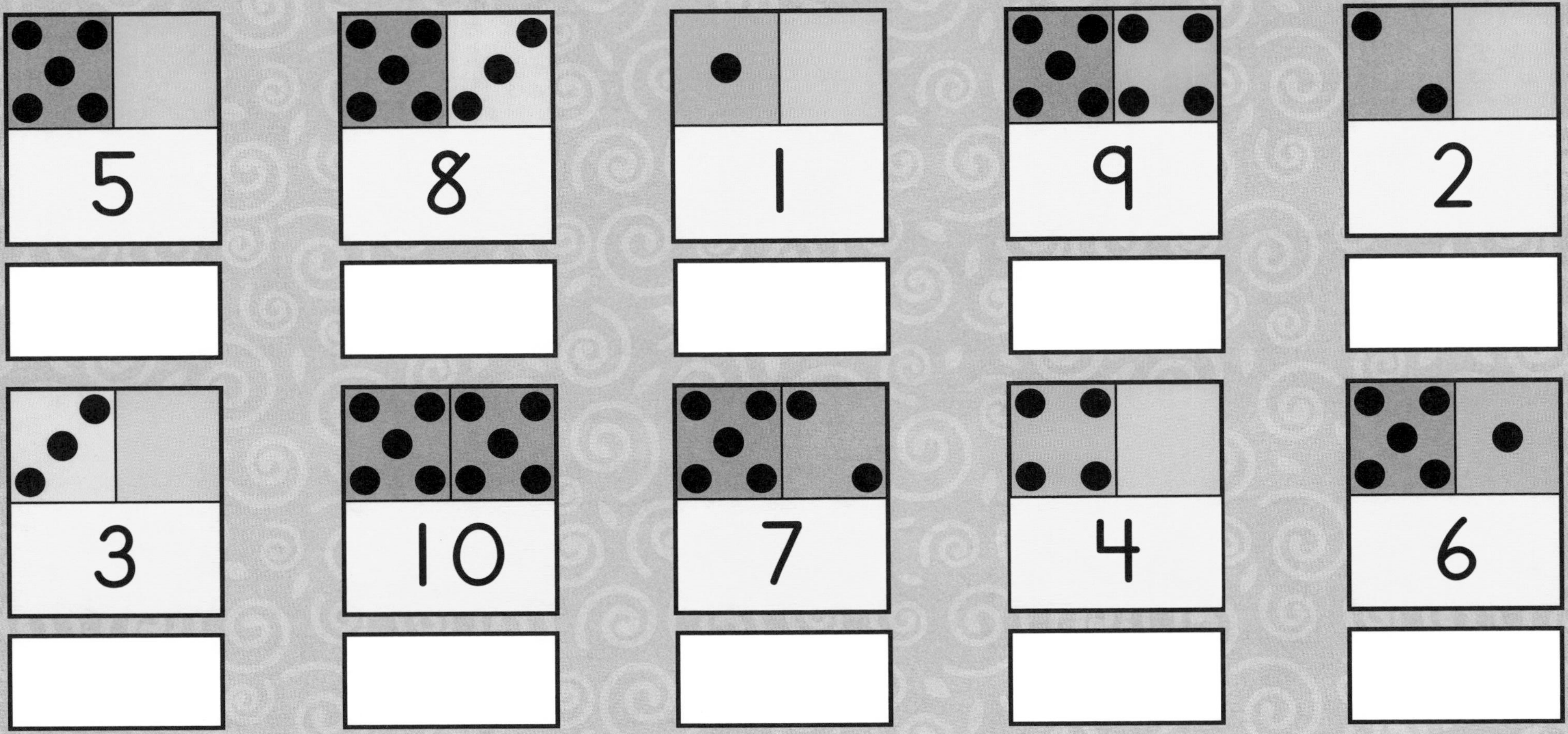

5		1		9		2
3		7		4		6
8		10				

one	nine	four	five	eight
two	three	ten	six	seven

Number Match Up

Cut out the number words and glue them in the box under the correct number picture.

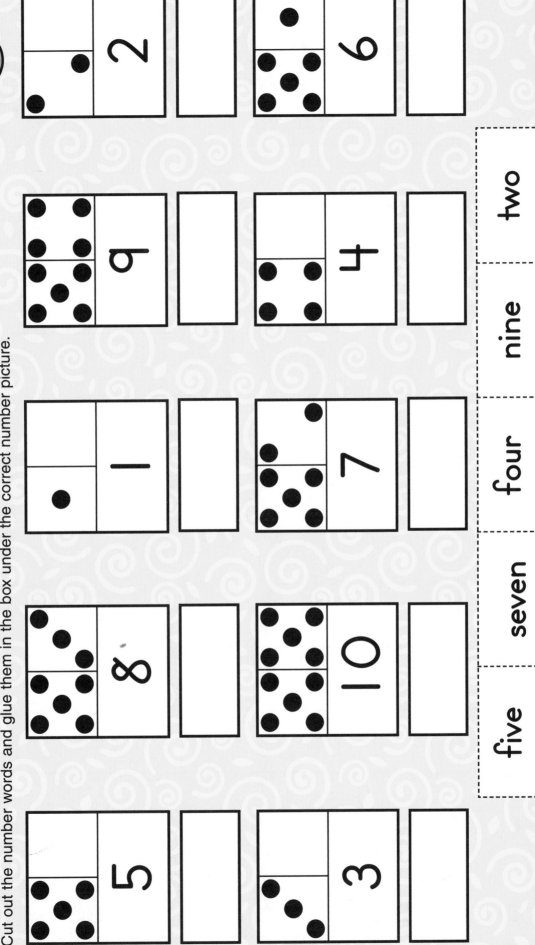

Order the Numbers

Cut out the number words. Paste them in order from one to ten. Then draw a matching number of objects in the space provided.

eight	five	four	nine	one
seven	six	ten	three	two

Name: _____

How Many Animals on the Farm?

Look at the picture. Fill in the blank with the correct number word to complete the sentences.

Number Words

one	three	five	seven	nine
two	four	six	eight	ten

There are _____ birds.

There are _____ pigs.

There is _____ horse.

There are _____ cats.

How Many Are There?

Draw a line from the number picture to the number word. Write the number word.

four

_____four_____

five

_____

two

_____

one

_____

three

_____

six

_____

seven

_____

Name: _____

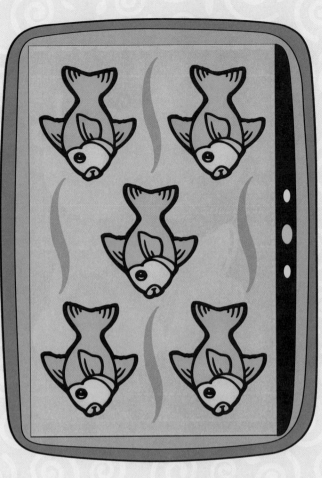

Number Words

Cut out the words and place them in the boxes to make a complete sentence. Read your sentence!

There were five fish.

There	were	five	fish.

Name: _____

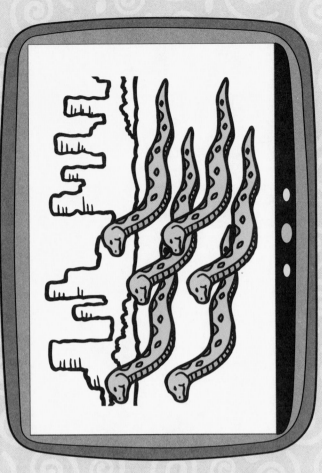

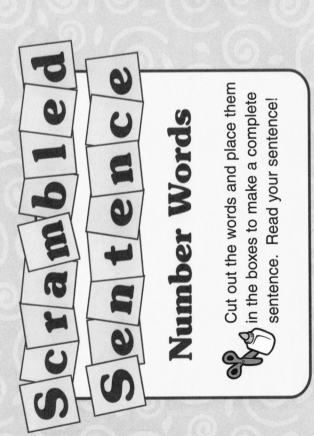

Scrambled Sentence

Number Words

Cut out the words and place them in the boxes to make a complete sentence. Read your sentence!

Six snakes will go.

Six	will	snakes
go.		

Name: _____

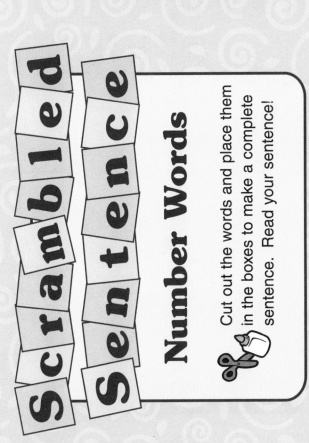

Number Words

✂ 🖊 Cut out the words and place them in the boxes to make a complete sentence. Read your sentence!

He has four brothers.

four	He	has	brothers.

80

Name: _____

 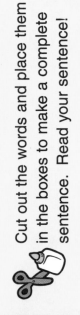

Number Words

Cut out the words and place them in the boxes to make a complete sentence. Read your sentence!

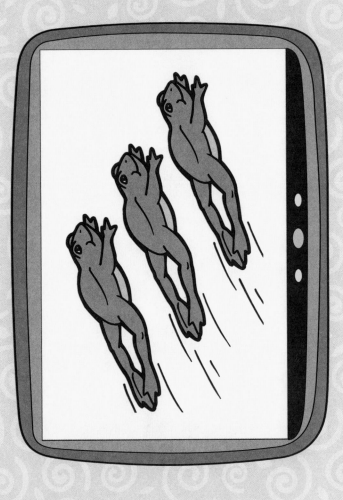

Three frogs will go up.

go	Three	up.	will	frogs

82

Name: _____

Scrambled Sentence

Number Words

Cut out the words and place them in the boxes to make a complete sentence. Read your sentence!

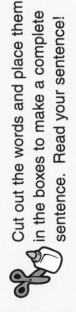

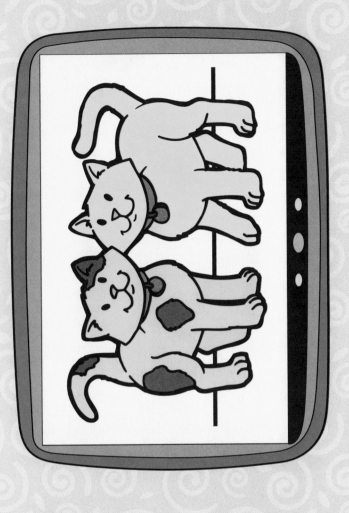

One of the cats is yellow.

One	yellow.	cats	of	the	is

84

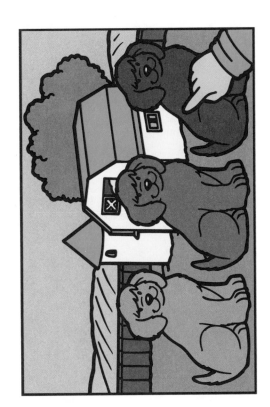

How Many Animals at the Farm?

By: _____

2

There are two goats at the farm.

1

There is one horse at the farm.

3

There are three dogs at the farm.

There are five pigs at the farm.

___

There are seven fish at the farm.

___

There are four cats at the farm.

___

There are six birds at the farm.

___

88

___

q

There are nine ants at the farm.

___

11

Whew!

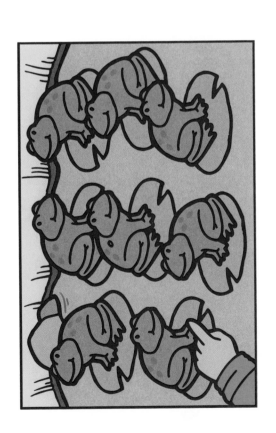

___

8

There are eight frogs at the farm.

___

10

But there are no snakes at the farm.

90

Shape and Position
Picture and Word Cards

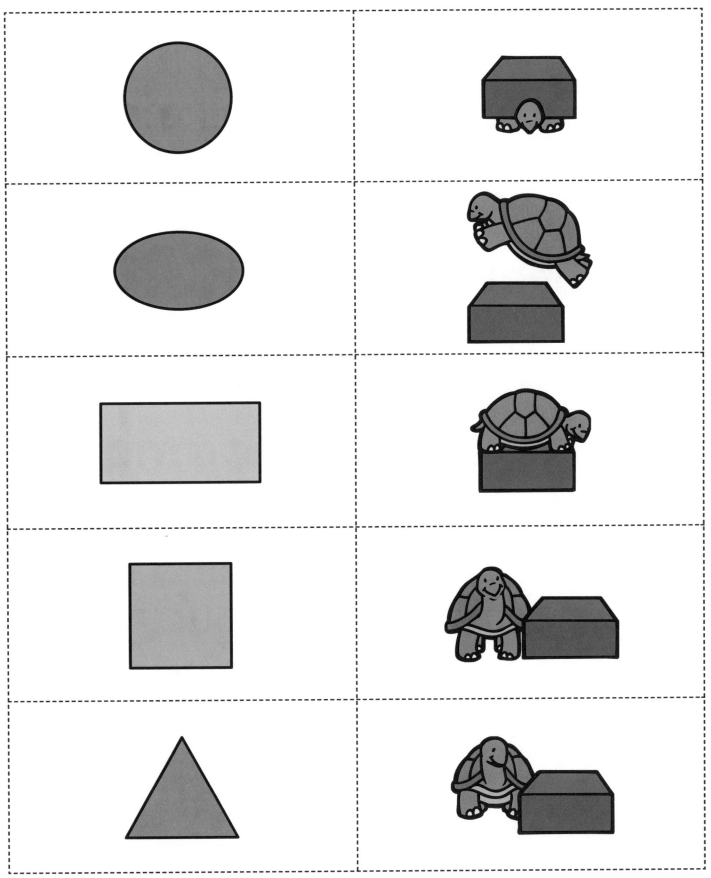

Shape and Position
Picture and Word Cards

under

circle

over

oval

on

rectangle

near

square

off

triangle

Shape and Position
Picture Cards

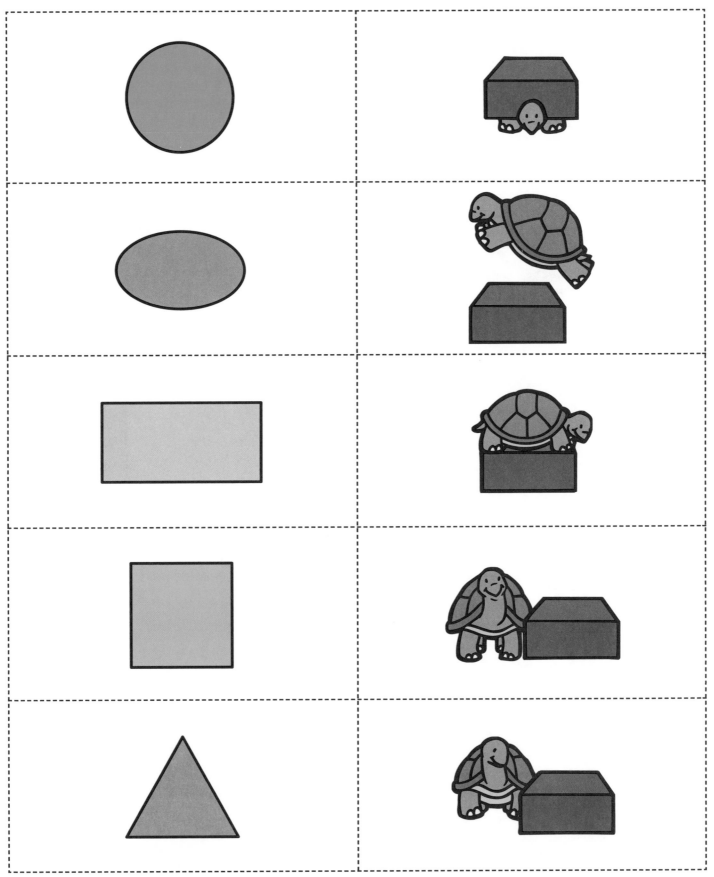

Shape and Position
Word Cards

circle	oval
rectangle	square
triangle	under
over	on
off	near

Name: _____

Shape and Position Match Up

Cut out the shape and position words and glue them in the box under the correct picture.

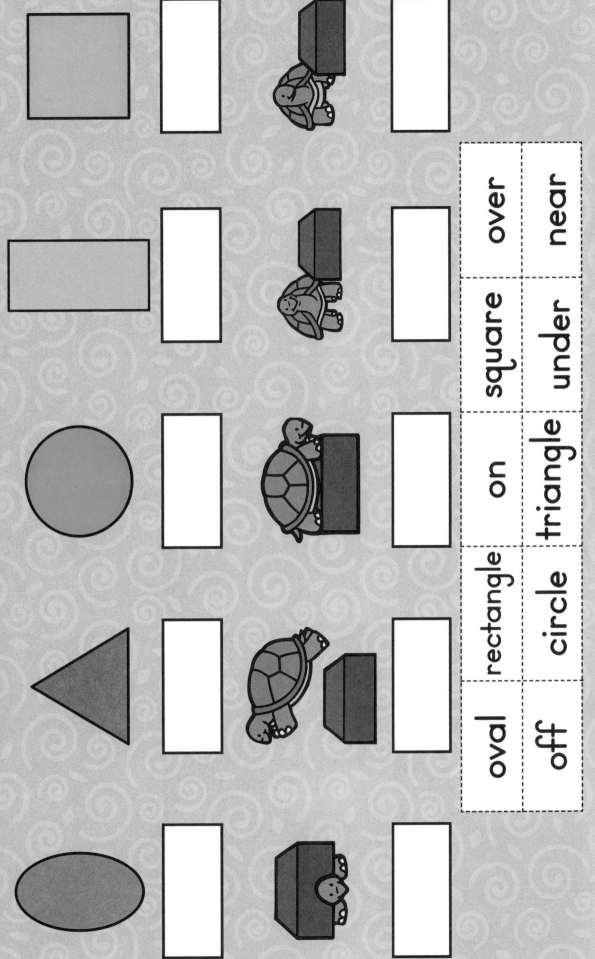

	over
near	
square	
	under
on	
triangle	
rectangle	
	circle
oval	
off	

Name: _____

Shape and Position Match Up

Cut out the shape and position words and glue them in the boxes under the correct pictures. Color the pictures.

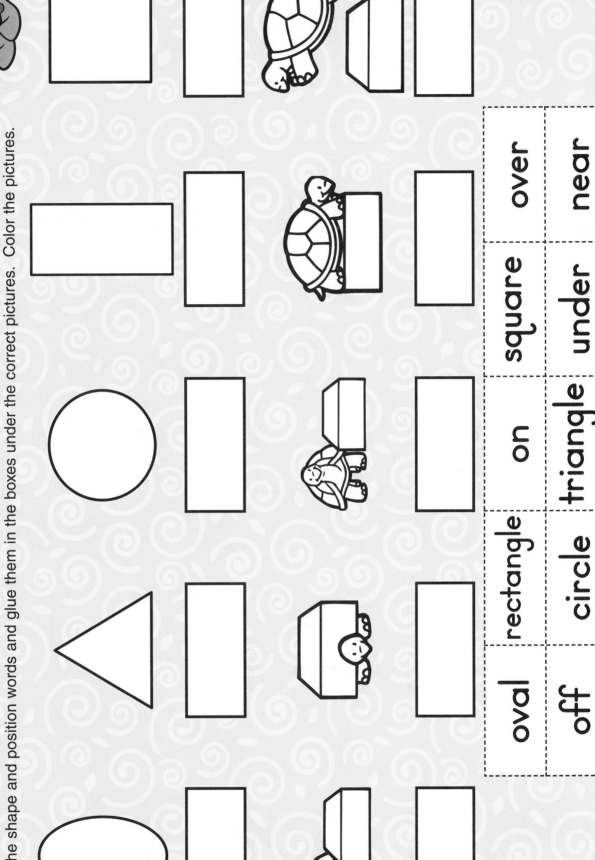

rectangle	on	square	over
oval	off	circle	triangle	under	near

Name: _____

Shape Up

Cut out the shapes and place them with their shape name.

circle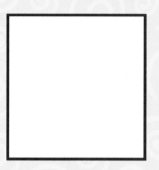

square

triangle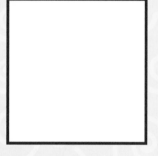

oval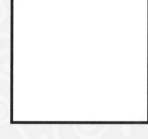

rectangle

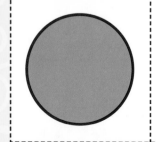  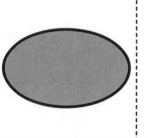  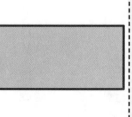

Name: _____

Find the Shape

Look at the picture. Fill in the blank with the correct shape word to complete the sentence.

circle   square   rectangle   triangle   oval

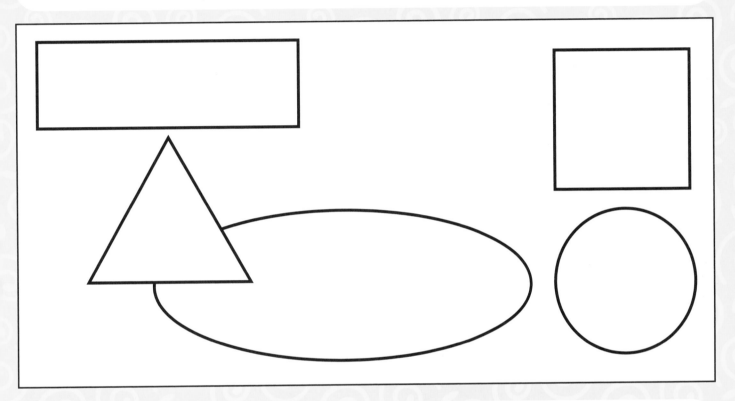

The _____ is on the _____ .

The _____ is near the _____ .

The _____ is over the _____ .

The _____ is under the _____ .

The _____ fell off the _____ .

Name: _____

Where Is It?

Read the position words. Fill in the correct position word in the sentences below.

| Position Words | on | over | near | under |

A hen is _____ the tree.

A bird is _____ the tree.

A dog is _____ the tree.

A cat is _____ the tree.

Name: _____

Scrambled Sentence

Shape and Position Words

Cut out the words and place them in the boxes to make a complete sentence. Read your sentence!

This square is orange.

square	is	This	orange.

104

Name: _____

Scrambled Sentence

Shape and Position Words

Cut out the words and place them in the box to make a complete sentence. Read your sentence!

The circle is over the square.

The	is		circle	square.	over	the

Name: _____

Shape and Position Words

Cut out the words and place them in the box to make a complete sentence. Read your sentence!

A goat is near the girl.

near	is	the	goat	girl.	A

Name: _____

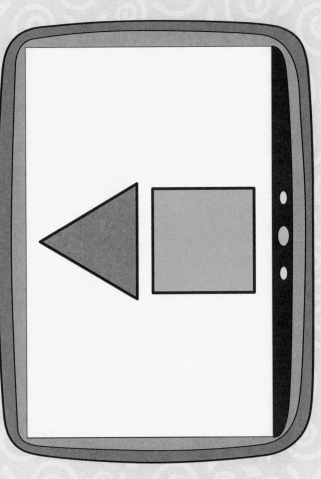

Scrambled
Sentence

Shape and Position Words

Cut out the words and place them in the box to make a complete sentence. Read your sentence!

The triangle is over the square.

the	over	triangle	square.	is	The

Name: _____

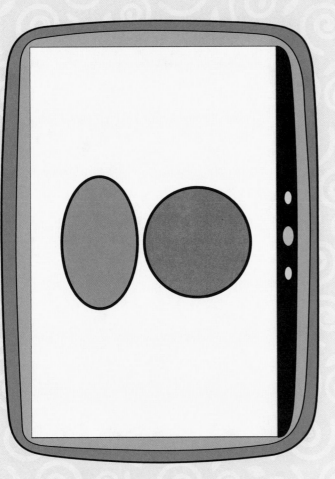

Shape and Position Words

Cut out the words and place them in the box to make a complete sentence. Read your sentence!

The circle is under the oval.

The	is	circle	oval.	under	the

Where Are the Shapes?

By: ___

1

Where is the circle? ___

2

The circle is over the square. ___

3

Where is the square? ___

5

Where is the rectangle?

___ ___

7

Where is the triangle?

___ ___

4

The square is under the circle.

___ ___

6

The rectangle is on the triangle.

___ ___

116

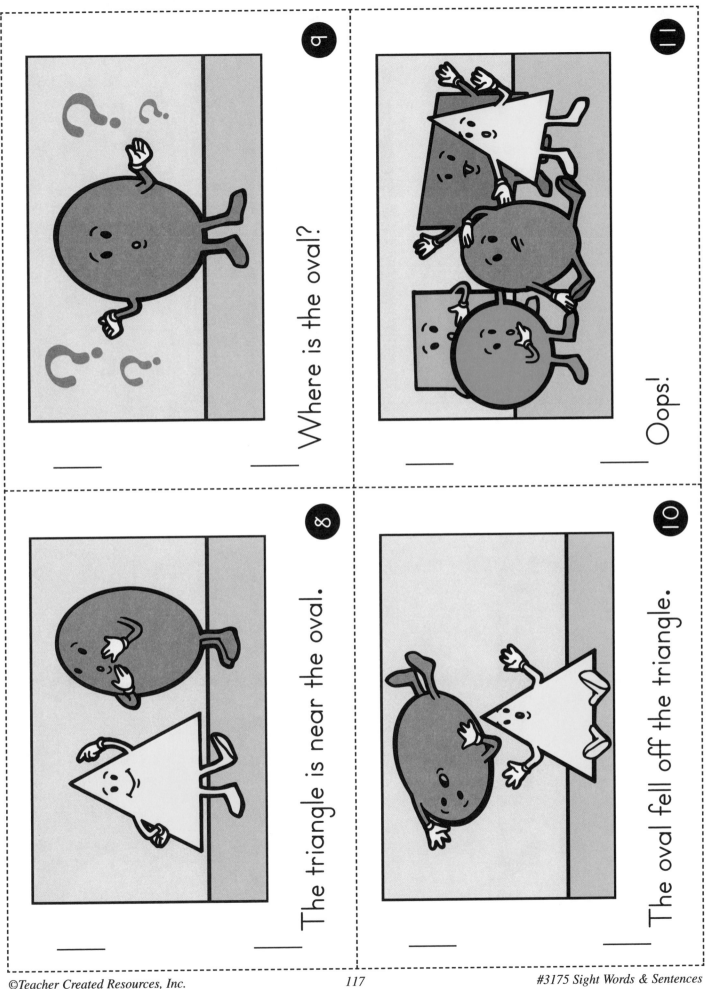

9

___ Where is the oval?

11

___ Oops!

8

___ The triangle is near the oval.

10

___ The oval fell off the triangle.

#3175 Sight Words & Sentences

Action Picture and Word Cards

Action Picture and Word Cards

jump

draw

play

look

run

read

sit

sing

write

walk

Action Picture Cards

Action Word Cards

draw	jump
look	play
read	run
sing	sit
walk	write

Name: _____

Action Word Match Up

Cut out the action words. Match the words to the correct action pictures.

read	look	run	sit	write
draw	jump	play	sing	walk

Action Word Match Up

Cut out the action words and glue them in the boxes under the correct action pictures. Color the pictures.

draw	read
jump	look
play	run
sing	sit
walk	write

Fill in the Action

Fill in the blanks to complete the sentences. Use the pictures for help.

| jump | look | read | run | sing | write |

The girl will _____ with a pencil.

He can sit and _____ the book.

He can _____ at it.

Look, she can _____ over it!

I can _____ fast.

She likes to _____.

Name: _____

What's the Action?

Circle the two words that are the same. Write the action word.

sing	song	sing _____
drip	draw	draw _____
walk	walk	with _____
like	look	look _____
run	run	rug _____
sit	sat	sit _____

Name:_____

Action!

Use one of the action words to write a sentence. Draw a picture.

draw	look	read	sing	walk
jump	play	run	sit	write

Name: _____

Action Words

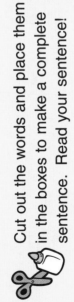

Cut out the words and place them in the boxes to make a complete sentence. Read your sentence!

We like to read!

to	We	like	read!

132

Name: _____

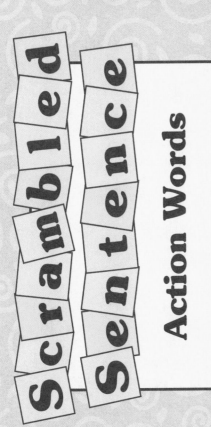

Scrambled Sentence

Action Words

Cut out the words and place them in the boxes to make a complete sentence. Read your sentence!

The green frog likes to jump.

likes	green	frog	The	to
			jump.	

134

Name: _____

Scrambled Sentence

Action Words

Cut out the words and place them in the boxes to make a complete sentence. Read your sentence!

She can draw and write.

draw	and	She	can	write.

Name: _____

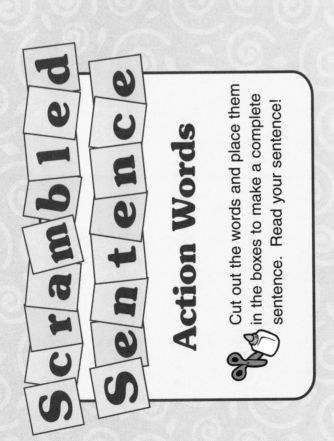

Action Words

Cut out the words and place them in the boxes to make a complete sentence. Read your sentence!

Can she walk over the snake?

walk	she	Can	over	snake?	the

138

Name: _____

Scrambled Sentence

Action Words

Cut out the words and place them in the boxes to make a complete sentence. Read your sentence!

We can jump and play.

We	play.	and	can	jump

140

1

We run at school.

___

3

We sing at school.

___

We Like School

___

By: ___

2

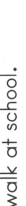

We walk at school.

___

We jump at school.

___ ___

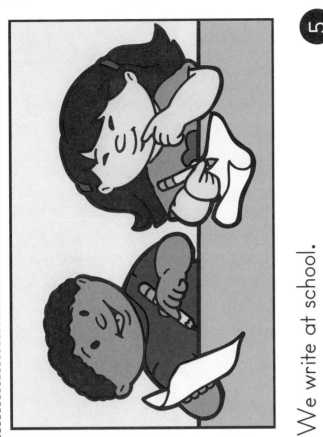

We write at school.

___ ___

We read at school.

___ ___

We draw at school.

___ ___

We play with balls at school.

____

We like school.

____

We play with blocks at school.

____

We look at books at school.

____

Question Word Cards

How?

Which?

What?

Who?

Why?

When?

Where?

???

???

???

Question Word Cards

How?

Which?

What?

Who?

Why?

When?

Where?

? ? ?

? ? ?

? ? ?

Name: _____

Party Time!

Cut out the information boxes at the bottom of the page. Put the information next to the correct question word.

Who?

What?

When?

Where?

| Monday at 12:00 p.m. | Kim White |
| Pizza Party | 1416 Lake Street |

Who, What, When, and Where

Cut out the question words at the bottom of the page. Put the question words next to the correct information on the invitation.

Monday at 12:00 p.m.

Kim White

1416 Lake Street

Pizza Party

Where?

Who?

What?

When?

Questions

Complete each sentence with the correct question word.

How	Which	Why	What

_____ color is it?

_____ shape is tall?

_____ many girls do you see?

_____ is he there?

Write a question.

_____

_____

Name: _____

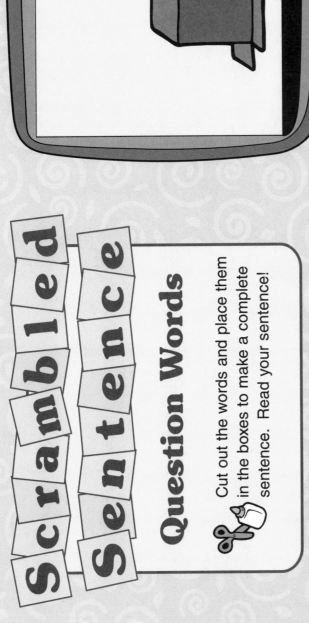

Scrambled Sentence

Question Words

✂ Cut out the words and place them in the boxes to make a complete sentence. Read your sentence!

What is under the box?

the	is	under	What	box?

Name: _____

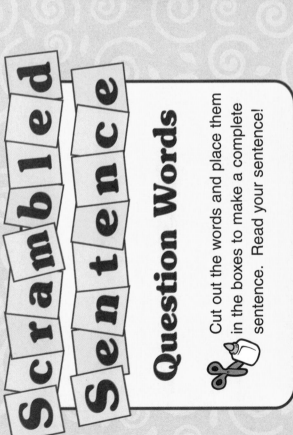

Question Words

Cut out the words and place them in the boxes to make a complete sentence. Read your sentence!

Where is the yellow bird?

Where	the	is	bird?	yellow

Name: _____

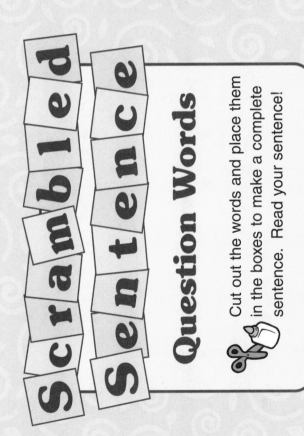

Scrambled Sentence

Question Words

Cut out the words and place them in the boxes to make a complete sentence. Read your sentence!

Which big dog is all brown?

all	big	dog	Which	is	brown?

Name: _____

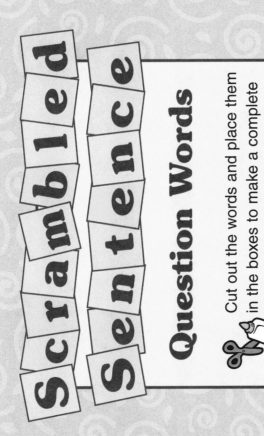

Question Words

Cut out the words and place them in the boxes to make a complete sentence. Read your sentence!

When can I go play?

When	go	can	play?	I

Name: _____

Scrambled Sentence

Question Words

Cut out the words and place them in the boxes to make a complete sentence. Read your sentence!

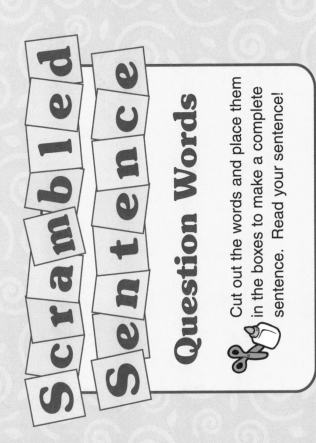

How many boys can sing?

boys	can	How	many	sing?

164

What is it? It's a party!

Where is it? It's here!

The Party

By: _____

When is it? It's today!

5

Everyone will come.

___

7

Which special day is it?

___

4

How many people will come?

___

6

Why is there a party?

___

168

9

Who is the party for?

___

11

HAPPY BIRTHDAY!

___

8

It's a birthday.

___

10

It's for you!

___

Animals

Animal Words

bird	dog	frog	hen	pig
cat	fish	goat	horse	snake

Name: _____

My Family

Family Words

baby	brother	family	mom
boy	dad	girl	sister

How Many?

Number Words

one	three	five	seven	nine
two	four	six	eight	ten

Shapes and Positions

Shape and Position Words

circle	rectangle	triangle	off	over
oval	square	near	on	under

Name: _____

Action

Action Words

draw	look	read	sing	walk
jump	play	run	sit	write

Questions, Questions

Question Words

how	what	when	where
which		who	why